THE
FRIENDSHIP
OF JESUS

*Also by John Woolley
and published by Arthur James*

I Am With You

Sorrow Into Joy

Prayers for the Family

Words of Power

God's Secret

THE
FRIENDSHIP
OF JESUS

John Woolley

ARTHUR JAMES
JOHN HUNT PUBLISHING
NEW ALRESFORD
1999

This edition first published in 1999 by

ARTHUR JAMES
an imprint of
JOHN HUNT PUBLISHING
46a West Street, New Alresford, Hants SO24 9AU
United Kingdom

Previously published in 1984 by Crown (Great Britain)

A catalogue record for this book is available
from the British Library.

ISBN 0 85305 447 9

Typeset in Adobe Goudy by
Strathmore Publishing Services, London N7

Printed and bound by
Tien Wah Press, Singapore

Contents

Introduction

Jesus.

Just look at that name for a moment. It's magnetic isn't it? If you're half-asleep, it wakes you up. If life has grown very dark for you, it seems to bring hope – even if it's only a flicker.

Jesus.

Keep looking at it for a second or two. In the whole world, it's the one name which refuses to be ignored. Whatever your background or personality, you find you're *interested*.

People look at Jesus in trying to make sense of a world containing so many cruel contradictions:

· The refugee with those haunted eyes.
· The sad little black child, only hours away from dying.
· The young person in the next street lying ill with cancer.

It's not surprising that so many feel God doesn't exist – or that if He does exist, He's just not interested in us. At the same time, you will find, everywhere, people who have a sort of instinct about Jesus. They're not completely sure about Him – but even just looking at His name they start to feel a bit more hopeful. There's a reason for this. Jesus is the only real hope of any person on this planet. (Big statement! We'll look at some of the reasons for it shortly.)

There's one thing absolutely certain: if anyone experiences the marvellous changes Jesus can make in a person's life, those arguments about whether He is divine become irrelevant! If Jesus shares your life, you know beyond a shadow of a doubt, that you've got God with you. You stop searching.

Is this you?

You may not remember when you were last inside a church – but you feel you'd like to know a lot more about Jesus. This book was written just for you.

Perhaps you are involved in a church – but are among the many who don't know Jesus in a warm and real way. This book was written just for you.

By the end of the book I have prayed that whatever your age or personal make-up, you'll be well on the way to knowing Jesus – I mean *really* knowing Him – as a friend. By the end of the book, I can almost hear you saying: 'I don't need a lot more reading or searching or wishing because I'm sure of Him!' This is because Jesus Himself will have been working in you – quite apart from your reading.

People in hospital were always asking me about Jesus (including many who were a bit frightened by organized religion!) – wanting to exchange that wistful longing for something better.

I wonder if you once had a strong faith – but you've almost lost it? I wonder if you have many problems in your life right now, and feel that it's *His* help you really need?

Well, together, we'll look very closely at Jesus – this person who lived on the earth at a definite time and place, and is now in charge of everything we see around us. You will start the exciting process of getting acquainted with Him. You will find out how to *enjoy* that relationship – whatever your personality. Yes, *enjoy* – even if you're thinking right now how many huge barriers exist!

You've realized of course that discovering the friendship of Jesus doesn't all depend on you. In fact, He has already taken the initiative – giving you a wish to know Him. So, if you've all sorts of misgivings, all sorts of conflicts, all sorts of problems, or if you're just among that huge number who can only say 'I wish …', here are two tremendous facts to get hold of:

1 Jesus does want you to know Him. He doesn't play hide-and-seek with people.
2 He does want you to *experience* how much He loves you.

Jesus wants to be, for you, not a cosy escape from life, but someone who is going to meet the hard realities of living with you. And this is going to make all the difference.

One to one!
There are always people frantically looking for an 'experience' of Jesus. Perhaps you, too, feel that He won't light up for you unless you find that dynamic service or inspiring meeting – as if He *needed* these occasions to break through.

You may be tempted to feel that if you try a bit harder, read a few more books, He'll seem more real. Well, I've got good news for you. You may not need to find the 'right' book, or the 'right' Christian friend, or the 'right' meeting.

There is one big step which so many people never get round to making. Will you take that step now – not worrying about the accompanying feelings as you do so!

Just ask Jesus (even if He seems rather remote at the time) to start sharing your life. He can't resist that request. Sharing your life is exactly what He'll start to do. You can then forget looking for that spectacular 'experience'. Jesus is going to work in His way – tailored just for you. You'll find that you're sharing all that *He* is – that you're part of Him. This isn't just fancy language, as you'll soon discover. Jesus will start to be real for you.

You'll find that you can feel calm, that you can feel strong, by just having a word with Him. You'll find that a sense of Jesus *with you* throughout each day is not reserved for those few super-spiritual people!

On a hospital ward, a patient often said something like this to me: 'I'm not very religious, Padre, but, you know, I always think of Jesus as a friend.' Yes, there's that word again. He's a super friend! He's never beaten by any circumstances. He's completely dependable. You'll find that the true experience of Jesus which is waiting for you doesn't start off with a bang and then leave you disappointed.

To be realistic, you don't, of course, escape from all life's difficult places if Jesus is your friend. But you'll notice something wonderful. You'll notice Him making everything fit into a pattern for you – in a way which only God can do.

Yes, you too

Countless books have been written, haven't they? Many describe dramatic healings, lives being changed, all sorts of spectacular and inspiring incidents. I wonder if you're one of the majority who, after putting down the book, feeling very sad, has thought: 'That's great – but why doesn't it happen to me?' Well, from now, you won't be one of those many 'struggling Christians' who feel that knowing Jesus, in a warm sort of way, must be reserved for after you're dead!

Every category of person needs Jesus – though some (like you) realize it more than others.

Here's Jane, aged 17. She was desperately shy and she felt guilty about almost everything. She had to 'spoil' everything for herself. Jesus's love put things right, slowly but surely.

Here's Peter – a sad, elderly clergyman. He once believed very eagerly, but had only a dead feeling inside, after some events which left him disillusioned. Jesus 'came back' to put things right for Peter.

Here's Elizabeth, aged 42. She had prayed so desperately, for so long, but only occasionally felt close to God. Then Jesus gave Elizabeth a sense of His love – which changed everything.

By the way, we won't be spending a long time on admittedly important things like reading the Bible, attending Church, and the various aspects of 'Christian doctrine'. These are dealt with by many others more expertly than I could do!

What we *are* going to do (and I suspect this is what you want) is:

1 Start learning to be very *aware* of Jesus.

2   Learn how to go through each day with a relaxing sense of His love.
3   Learn how to start receiving His unique help for those, often desperate, needs and problems – things you may hide from those closest to you!

May I ask one favour? Forget about other people's spiritual 'success stories'. Forget all your previous disappointments – and look forward to experiencing Jesus sharing your life.

Your priority?

I think a pause would be useful right here, don't you? Could you, after a deep breath, promise yourself one thing? Promise yourself that knowing Jesus is going to be your top priority.

As you know, there was once the Great Train Robbery in Britain. One man – the head of the Flying Squad (Tommy Butler) – became obsessed with finding those responsible. He made countless trips abroad, missed many meals, went on hundreds of false leads – but never gave up. When he had just brought one more of the train robbers from the USA, a newspaper commented: 'Tommy Butler is the most dedicated cop in the business.' He had a ruling passion. He was in deadly earnest.

Shall I tell you something? The happiness of knowing Jesus as Friend comes to those who put this *desire* for Him first – and keep it, in spite of perhaps years of disappointments. This is the way it happened for me – changing my whole life. And this is the way I'm sure it's going to happen for you.

But who *is* Jesus? It's natural to ask this, because so many who influence opinion in the Church, who appear on TV, or who write books, hold such frighteningly different beliefs about Him! So we'll take a look at Him now.

When working among hospital patients I saw many prayers answered.

As a reader of this book, there has been a prayer said for you. It is that you will know, unmistakeably, the companionship of Jesus – even if you've been at a 'wistful' stage for a long, long time!

I know that it's going to be a *lasting* friendship – long after you've finished the book.

CHAPTER I

Who *Is* Jesus?

'I can admire Him but ...'

'I suppose He's the greatest person who ever lived.'

'I can't believe all that the Bible says about Him, just because fairy-tales are pleasant.'

Here you are in this vast, apparently impersonal, puzzling universe. If a voice whispered, 'Behind all this, I assure you, there is a loving God,' there are times when you might not be convinced!

'Believers' seem to fall, very roughly, into two categories.

The first group put Jesus on a pedestal. He is God. He has all things in His hands. Watching Jesus walking about Palestine, people were looking at the God of this universe incredibly revealed in a human life.

Then there is a second group. While believing in God, they are not too sure about

Jesus being all He claimed to be, or was reported to be.

And so how does Jesus fit into a universe in which we say, 'There is a God who loves us,' but which contains so much that is frightening or meaningless? For the honest person, the two seem so hard to reconcile, don't they?

Well, in this sort of world, don't you feel glad, as I do, that we've heard the name Jesus? You will have guessed that I'm not with those in the second group. I regard Jesus as supreme in the whole scheme of creation. Knowing what He has come to mean to me, and to so many that I used to meet in the wards of our hospitals, I couldn't do otherwise! In Jesus we experience all we will ever need to experience of God. God the Father's tremendous love just shines through Jesus His Son – as much of that love as we could ever want.

They're one!

Using some cameras, you have to twiddle a knob until two images coincide. When they do, you're in focus. It's so sad that there are many people today who have two religious 'images'. First, there's God, the

Father, the Creator. Secondly, there's Jesus, whom they feel may or may not have been God revealed in human form.

It is when these images 'God' and 'Jesus' coincide that religion starts to become excitingly alive! God our Father becomes real and close to you when you find Him in Jesus. Yes, I know it could be dangerous to confuse them, forgetting that there is a Father and there is a Son. *But both are God.* The real danger comes when they become 'split' – or when Jesus is slightly demoted, as so often happens today.

If you had a chance to eavesdrop on one or two people of deep faith saying their prayers, you'd find that the words 'Father' and 'Jesus' are used interchangeably to-wards the Person they are addressing.

Before those increasingly complex creeds were composed, the very early Christians seem to have had just one phrase by which they lived: 'Jesus is Lord'. For practical, working purposes, God was the God they saw in Jesus. Karl Barth, a giant among theologians, puts it this way: 'From the very start, in trying to think of God we've just got to think of Jesus Christ.' But many people today tend to push Jesus on one side with a big question mark over Him. And then they go on to say how sure they feel about God! It just doesn't work.

Jesus said to His friends in Palestine: 'If you've seen Me, you've seen God.' How about that! Think of what this means for you if you want Him to be your friend and companion. It's in Jesus that we see God *defined* in all His love and power.

Listen to an Indian doctor – bright blue turban, black beard, as he takes a few minutes off from the ward to ask about becoming a Christian: 'If you believe in God, what better way could anyone imagine of Him revealing Himself, than in a human life?' Exactly, Dr Singh! You non-Christians are often more truly Christian than some of us 'professionals'!

He did it!

Have I perhaps been making it sound a bit too simple or too patronizing? – because after all, people have studied for centuries the complex question of just how the divine and human natures could meet in Jesus.

Well, even if the 'how' of it is rather puzzling, it is perfectly reasonable just to accept that *God did it* – that He showed us Himself, perfectly, in Jesus. If He didn't, I think I'd find it very difficult to believe in God in a universe like this, wouldn't you?

God, in fact, is not that unknowable 'wholly-other' being whom many sadly feel they have got to accept. We look at Jesus and discover what a wonderful God we've got, after all.

Rather like that little girl, blind from birth, who had the bandages removed after a successful operation, saw her father smiling down at her and said: 'Just to think I've had a lovely dad like that all along.'

So why not see yourself in Group Number One – ready to believe the very best of Jesus? If you do, the whole business of 'God' is going to come to life for you. I know that this is what Christianity is *supposed* to be all about – but sometimes you wonder what has happened!

The 'bigger' your view of Jesus, the more you're going to expect from Him. And with Jesus – just to show that He *is* God – you're not going to be disappointed.

It's always worth keeping firmly in mind that when Jesus began life in that smelly stable, this was *God* breaking into our world and experiencing, in the closest possible way, all the hopes and all the heartbreaks of being human.

The New Testament, as you know, comes from a wide variety of writers – but you can't escape the message which runs right through: that Jesus is over all things – past, present and future.

Now I realize that you will want to use your reason courageously. You won't want to hide from facts and create a fairy-tale Jesus. But the remarkable thing is that countless people using the reasoning method about Jesus, have ended up sure that He *is* someone on whom they can pin all their hopes.

You, too, can look forward to the time when all the arguments stop and there comes the certainty that Jesus is all that His loved ones through the centuries have said that He is.

I've been allowed to see Jesus do many wonderful things for people. But what I'm interested in now is Jesus doing something, not for them, but for *you*.

Friend plus

Is 'Friend' just a sentimental and reassuring title, helping us to escape a little from the realities of life? Is it a pleasant fantasy which has nothing to do with what life is all about?

To have a true human friend is, of course, one of the most relaxing things. You don't have to pretend with that friend. That friend is concerned about you, shares with you, wants your best interests. But there will be many reading this who don't have a human friend in that category.

So what about the friendship of Jesus?

That friendship is all the things we've just thought about – but so much more. There's permanence (our loved ones or friends may be lost, of course); there's knowledge of our past, present and future – with a resultant wisdom which will always plan what is best for us. There is all the power and majesty of God.

I have thé feeling that you're not going to give up now. If so, congratulations!

Dear Lord,
I'm aware of many doubts – about You,
and about myself. I can't hide from You that
often I'm unsure of Your existence.
And yet I feel that truly to know Your
friendship is the best thing this life can offer.
So please let me know You,
above everything else, as my Friend.
Thank You.

CHAPTER TWO

Just Love!

People often forget that the friendship of Jesus really depends upon one thing. I'm sure you have guessed what it is. He doesn't become our Friend because of our good works, our virtue, our churchgoing, our determination, the amount of *faith* we can produce.

You're ahead of me! You've already guessed what is the big factor. Yes, it all depends upon the *love* of Jesus. Let's think about it for a few moments.

There are those who come to feel the warmth of Jesus's love deeply. But, sadly, there are many others who, though they 'believe', do not feel His love for them at all. Many people have areas deep within where God is anything but love. At this deep level, there can be a feeling that He often treats His children worse than we treat our own. And so, although a person may outwardly protest, 'Of course, God is love,' it doesn't always find an echo in the very deepest part of that person.

On this shaky foundation, many go on to build a life of trying to 'serve Him', 'helping the Church', which often becomes a grim business.

And so, task number one – and it's a pleasant one! Start thinking, as never before, about the indescribable love of Jesus, our Lord. See it in His life on earth. See it in the way He let Himself be killed for you and me. Look and look at that love – until it begins to sink deep into you.

And it does sink down, whatever those 'barriers' of yours. Deep inside you, God's Spirit is going to be working. And you'll become increasingly sure of Jesus's love for you.

Hold on a moment!

'Surely Christianity is not all about going around with a cosy sense of His love! What about the practical job of just doing what He tells us?' This is a down-to-earth member of the church down the road, who'll be popping up occasionally during the rest of our book – he's Adrian.

What Adrian is failing to realize is that those who really experience the love of Jesus every day, *want* to please Him more than anything else.

In other words, 'doing what He tells us' coming naturally – rather than the grim (often resentful) 'obedience' and 'good works' of those who don't feel His love.

It's vital to allow *plenty of time* to think about the love of Jesus before 'finding His will' or asking 'what form shall my service for Him take?' So could we consider one or two things? They will sound pretty familiar, but it's surprising what can happen to you when you really focus on them:

1   The love flowing from Jesus (which is the love of God our Father) just could not be stronger.
2   That love is lasting love. He is not capricious.
3   He *longs* for us to know that love.
4   His dearest wish is our *happiness*.

I wonder if you are one of those who feel that they don't deserve His love? (A lot of people I talk to feel this way.) If you are, may I say:

· He, in fact, thinks the world of you – in spite of all you may think about yourself.
· He accepts you, with all your imperfections – which is why He is so much greater than often our consciences are!

People, in reaching out for God, have often been led to think, 'I must go and be useful for such-and-such a church,' and 'I must make some promises to Him.' They might have been wiser to spend a day or two just telling themselves *'He loves me!'* Though it appears that religion has been made very complex, it isn't really. It all hangs on those three little words.

So don't rush this vital stage of thinking about how much Jesus our Lord loves you. Don't be over-anxious for the moment, about what you feel you 'ought' to be doing for Him. Don't be anxious, even, about those personal needs with which you desperately want Him to deal!

Just let His love be *very* much in your thoughts. As you do so, the foundation is being built for His friendship to be experienced in increasingly exciting ways.

Dear Lord,
Please let me have a deep awareness of Your
love – and let our friendship grow from this.
Thank You.

CHAPTER THREE

What His Friendship Brings

Just a few moments to look at some things which happen if Jesus is your Friend. By the way, if you decide to seek *His* friendship, it's going to settle a lot of conflicts about smaller decisions in the future!

It means that you begin to give all your concerns from your often uncertain hands into His very sure ones. It means that even when your situation is far from perfect, you're still going to enjoy Him with you.

Thinking of His love, you'll begin to relax a little. You'll begin to put your trust – not in your efforts, your 'status' or your achievements, but in what *He* is.

It will seem as if nothing in your life is outside Jesus any more. He will influence your thinking, conversations, decision-making. You'll be calm – and with a growing feeling that you're never alone. As the sense of the friendship deepens, you'll almost enjoy uncertain situations because you're meeting them with Him!

You're going to find that instead of tense efforts at 'being virtuous', there'll be a new self – a Jesus-filled self. *How much a person misses, until he or she sees that living close to Jesus is much more about receiving and trusting than it is about trying frantically!*

Those situations which used to send you to pieces – you're going to meet them successfully. You'll find yourself taking for granted that Jesus is in every situation before you reach it – and a wonderful thing happens. You become increasingly aware of 'adverse circumstances' actually being made to work for a good purpose – sometimes many times in a day. You'll find doors opening, things 'happening', you'll find people coming (or *not* coming!). If Jesus really shares your life, He draws together all its complex interests and activities.

You?
I wonder if you're inclined to be shy, looking inwards a lot? With Jesus you begin to look away from yourself and your conflicts, and increasingly at *Him*. This makes a huge difference in your life, as you can guess.

Ask some of those who didn't used to sleep very well! There's one tremendous thing about Jesus. He always helps us to believe in ourselves. And because of this, you'll start to find a quiet joy of a sort you never had before – even at those times you used to call 'pleasure', even if you're hardly the dynamic or extrovert type!

Just a second to look at three people with whom Jesus was in contact:

1 Zaccheus, tax collector, made a very undignified ascent of a tree to see Jesus.
2 A woman with a long-standing illness pushed through a crowd, just to touch His clothes.
3 A paralysed man, with friends' help, got himself to Jesus the hard way – through the roof.

They all 'meant business', didn't they? And because of this, *something happened.* So don't forget that priority will you?

I'm pretty sure that your wish is to deeply experience Jesus's friendship. If so, you can be sure about one thing – the process has *already begun.* And He's got so much to give you!

Dear Lord,
I may have misgivings, but I am going to
expect the very best from you. Please help
me, because I know you want me really to
enjoy your friendship – always.
Thank You.

CHAPTER FOUR

Just Accepting!

This is probably the most difficult chapter in the book to write – because you're unique! It mustn't sound as if the friendship of Jesus depends on your going through some sort of formula. You don't have to find the right words, in order to 'capture' Him!

Jesus wants to grant your wish to know His love, in a way which will be indelible in your mind. He wants to do it in a way which will stand up to those swings of mood and sudden changes in your circumstances, which lie ahead. So you've got to be pretty sure, on looking back, of what you thought and did at the time of really accepting His friendship.

You may have asked yourself the sort of questions which follow. They're worth asking, if you've never done so.

Here they are:

1 Do I really want Jesus, not just as a
   helpful influence, or because of some
   specific need, or as a means of self-
   improvement – but as a friend, who can
   do absolutely what He wants with me?

2 Can He look at me and really know that
   He has *all* of me – ambitions, the future
   – everything? Can He?

3 Am I prepared, not just to enjoy the
   comforting sense of His love, but to face
   some of the not-so-pleasant things in
   myself?

4 Am I prepared to go with Him, perhaps
   through strange places, knowing that
   the only tragic thing in life is to walk
   alone – in the *wrong* direction?

When you consciously accept for yourself the love and friendship of Jesus, it's
often accompanied by a desperate sense of
'needing something'. Sometimes too, it's
accompanied by a sort of abandonment –
a throwing away of yourself, because you
need Him so much.

Brian Hession was a brave man who
inspired many who knew him by his
wonderful faith, while under sentence of
death with cancer. He once said that the

most important step in the life of a Christian was the one in which he or she just 'went flop' in the presence of Jesus.

Yes, just dropping all our images, our pretences, and telling Him how very much we need Him. He loves to hear that!

I know you'll expect God to deal with each one of us in a distinctive way. Here's John – usually a confident, very self-sufficient person. He may be brought to a position of seeing how little he has without God, or how much he needs the forgiveness of God. Here's Susan – she rather expects everything to happen fatalistically and passively. She may find Jesus leading her into letting herself influence events a bit more!

Be there!
You'd be surprised how helpful it is to find somewhere where you can be undisturbed and to think for a while about Jesus on the Cross. Just 'be there' in your imagination, at the greatest moment in all history. See them all – the soldiers, the sarcastic priests. In that moment Jesus saved a world which had cut itself off from God. Try reading the description of the Crucifixion in one of the Gospels, even if you think you know the

story well. Try, for example, reading Luke's version – with no rush.

As you're thinking about all this, it's worth remembering that because God transcends time, He already knew you and me during that event in Palestine!

Usually as you look at the incredible love of Jesus on the Cross, you can't help making it very personal and realizing 'He did that for *me*'. Did what? Well, He *took upon Himself* those callous and unloving ways I often find in myself. Jesus, so to speak, stood in the place of those alienated from God by their wrong-doing. His anguished cry of 'Why have You forsaken Me?' was His own sad experience of that separation.

There are some people, who, when thinking about Jesus on the Cross, even seem to hear Him gently speaking their name. No, it's not a morbid exercise! It's just a marvellous realization of how much He loves His children. Whenever we look at the Cross in this way, it seems to make larger the place which Jesus has in our hearts. (It's something you'll probably be doing quite often, in the future.) Looking at the Cross can easily make a person say something like: 'I'm deeply sorry, Lord, for all that has been wrong.' By the way, this isn't to be labelled 'confession' as if part of a formula! It's something spontaneous when wanting really to know His friendship. If our sorrow for all that has hurt Him is absolutely genuine, and if there is a sincere wish to change for the better, forgiveness just pours out of Jesus our Lord. We also find that His love helps us to forgive ourselves – not always easy for some!

All this means that those days of feverishly trying are on the way out.

There's one request which Jesus finds irresistible. It's when we ask Him that we might learn really to love Him. Loving a supernatural being, of course, is hardly the easiest thing in the world! But I can assure you that it happens to every type of person you could imagine.

Loving Him so often grows out of *gratitude*. He's so patient with us in those early unsure stages. We just can't help being grateful – and love for Him just can't help growing.

When Jesus said, 'Ask and you'll receive',

it wasn't just to sound pleasant. *He meant what He said.*

Do you feel that you're not the type of person who could ever succeed in knowing Jesus's friendship? I know I did. But it happened. And it's starting to happen for you, too. Don't rely on your words, but on His love. Be absolutely sure that if you've asked Him to share your life, that request is granted. Life is going to be very different for you from now on.

Don't feel that the little prayer following is essential – as long as you know you want His friendship with all your heart. It is printed in case anyone would like to borrow a phrase which expresses what they want to say. I know He is going to bless you very much.

Dear Lord,
Here I am, with all my shortcomings, my
fears, my current problems, my unfulfilled
longings and dreams. Please take me, and
start to make me what You want me to be.
I am deeply sorry for all that has been wrong
in my life. Please forgive me. Please help my
love for you to grow – and, Lord, I gladly
accept Your friendship now. I thank You that
there is going to be a growing awareness of
Your love – and that You will be exerting a
good influence upon me all the time.
Lord, I am so pleased that you are
my Friend – for ever.
Thank You.

CHAPTER FIVE

Just Walking!

Someone once wrote a little verse about a bear cub, who was very anxious about how to walk for the first time. He went on and on about this to his mother – should he put his right paw in front of the left, or the other way round? Mother said, 'Don't talk – just walk!'

So here we are! Did you ask Jesus to share your life and be your friend always? If you did, should you be expecting to feel ecstatic? Well, most people aren't instantly ten feet off the ground at this stage. In fact you may not notice any dramatic change just yet. But hold on a moment – some-thing *is* going to happen for you now. You're going to be steadier. You're going to be calmer. You're going to be more certain about Jesus and all that He is. And *real* joy is on the way. Are you tempted to read one more book? Or to hear one more talented speaker? Perhaps – but this could start you off 'wanting' again – when the time has arrived, in fact, for you to start 'just walking' with Jesus as your Friend.

Just walking – knowing that *you now share all that Jesus is*. And what's more, even in the early hesitant days you start living in heaven. This may sound a bit fanciful but it's true. Jesus Himself showed us how it's done – although admittedly He's a rather exceptional example! In Palestine, as you know, His feet were very firmly on the ground. He wasn't playing a part, but experiencing all the limitations of being a human being. He wasn't dreamy or detached from life. He knew the real world with all its poverty. He mixed with people where life was cheap, life was cruel. But because of His union with God the Father, His Body was on earth and His Spirit in heaven. It's a life of this kind which is offered to all who have Jesus as their friend. And you'll enjoy it more and more with each week that goes by!

Just walking. You want this friendship to be *real*. Well, nothing will make it more real than being absolutely honest. 'Lord, You do seem so remote at times' is *genuine* prayer.

Don't allow yourself even to slightly pretend, or to say the 'right' things.

Honesty with Jesus is so relaxing. We usually want to be honest with someone who loves and understands us anyway. Such honesty begins to make Him feel wonderfully close. That 'Lord, You seem so remote' won't need to be said so often. As we talk to Him regularly, of course, the feeling that we're talking to ourselves begins to disappear.

Just walking, you'll start to 'look' at Jesus in a natural and effortless way. You'll become almost afraid to start on anything without a realization (however brief) of Jesus with you. You're going to remember Him before every meeting, every conversation. Remembering that heavenly dimension to your life will become habitual.

You'll start giving that quick trusting glance to your Friend, even in the busiest, most absorbing situations.

This isn't to make Him 'do' things for you. What it does, though, is to help you *keep an awareness* of His companionship.

As you start 'just walking', remind

yourself as often as you can, that Jesus is your Friend – for keeps. It may once have sounded too good to be true – but that is what has happened.

Your one fixed point through the rest of your life is this: '*I belong to Him*'.

Getting started

Well now, what about the average day? (If there is such a thing!) Aren't those earliest moments often make or break? One witty person commented that some people wake with, 'Good morning, God!' and others, 'Good God ... morning!'

It's essential to give those very first moments to Jesus, your Friend. Many long-standing Christians fail to do this. In those earliest moments, as you know, your current anxieties and preoccupations usually start to pop into your mind. Whether or not you're feeling very 'spiritual', this is the time to do two things:

1 *Thank* Him for bringing you to the start of this day.
2 *Give* the day to Him.

Just that, for the moment.

Of course, there will be those who are so tired of living, that to face another day is something they would rather not do.

Giving the day to Jesus our Lord may seem a pretty formal habit, but in fact you can be absolutely sure that He is going to bless and use that day. Yes, He'll do it, even though we may be aware of still falling into the old ways.

For most people there is little time at the start of the day for 'being with' the Lord and telling Him what's in our hearts. But the thought of Him can nevertheless be there. It might be giving Him a two-second thought, or whispering His Name as we go downstairs to switch on the kettle. This keeps us focused on *Him* in this early part of the day, which is so important.

This awareness of Jesus stops all sorts of upsetting or trivial thoughts rushing in and spoiling the mood of the whole day.

I'm sure you'll find a moment just to promise Him to try, with His help, to live in the way you know He would approve. Here's something which will help:

Imaginatively meet the day with Jesus. 'See' yourself being calm, concerned about others you meet, not reacting with resentment, and so on. As we foresee the day with Him in this way, it increasingly works out the way we have previewed it. Allowing a few minutes for a quiet time, while caressing our mug of tea or coffee, is always well repaid.

Well, for most of us, that's it! There's breakfast, children to school perhaps, the rush to work. But there's no reason why Jesus should be very far from your thoughts. I know that you'll be watching for opportunities of breaking off for a second or two, so that you can just 'be with' Him in those thoughts.

Dear Lord,
You know about my duties, and the people
who may depend on me very much.
Please show me opportunities in each day
to just be quiet in Your presence.
Thank You.

CHAPTER SIX

Just Thinking!

Those times when you can be alone with Jesus each day soon become times you just wouldn't miss. They're going to make such a difference to the quality of your day. These times should start *early* in the friend-ship, by the way – not something you learn after belonging to a church for ten years!

'Prayer' can be a frightening word – it is to some very active Christians! It takes so many forms, but there's one thing I hope you'll find time to include somewhere in your day – a time of 'just thinking' about Jesus. We won't give this the grand title of Adoration or Contemplation. It's simply something we do which helps such a lot in deepening our awareness of His presence. It's even more helpful if there's no other aim than thinking about Him.

For example, perhaps you start thinking about how much Jesus loves you. It's natural to want to pass on from there to what else comes from being in His presence – His peace, His healing, His guidance, and so on. That's fine. Nothing wrong with that. And yet there will be times when just the thought of how much He loves you will be enough.

In other words, simply to enjoy your Friend, rather than some of the gifts, or the much-needed 'results' of that friendship.

There'll be times, of course, when you're feeling very agitated – perhaps unable to sit down and think at all. More than anything, you'll want the calm which the sense of His love brings. He understands perfectly our need of the things which flow from Him.

Don't have too many rules or 'patterns' – just as long as *He* is in your thoughts.

Let us say we've managed to steal two or three minutes apart with Jesus our Friend. It's a short time, but we find that He helps it to seem so calm and so unhurried. We can use a reflection along these lines – varying the words as we wish:

Lord I think of all that You are ...

Your love:
- *never changing*
- *so very patient*
- *so compassionate*

Your wisdom:
- *the exactness of Your ways*
- *Your perfect 'timing'*
- *the way in which You can harmonize the circumstances of my life*

Your greatness:
- *literally everything in Your control*
- *nothing can happen which is not within Your will*
- *only You can make difficult situations serve a good purpose*

However you may have been feeling when you started your time of quiet, you find that your reflection about Him brings a change for the better. It is this trust in all that He is, which increasingly becomes part of our thinking. It spills over from the few minutes we spend with Him into the rest of our life.

Wasted time?

Remember Adrian? Our down-to-earth member of the local church is here again. 'Now look,' he says, 'is the friendship with Jesus all about sitting down and "drinking Him in"?'

No, of course it isn't, Adrian. Most of our lives would not allow it anyway. But the daily walk with our Friend *is* very much about Jesus never being far from our thoughts.

Things have gone seriously wrong through great activity 'in His Name', but not very much thought given to *Him*! The greatest act of service for Jesus (so often neglected) is *to give Him our attention*.

People often ask what they should visualize at times of thinking about Jesus. You may already have worked this out. Some have in their minds their own image of our Lord as He was on earth. Some glance at a favourite picture, just to stimulate their imagination; others merely visualize an 'aura of loving kindness'. It will vary from person to person anyway. The point is that imagination grows up into faith, so that we come to feel very close to Him – with or without our 'image'.

Is thinking about Jesus a cosy escape from reality – after which we're brought down to the *real* world – where people can be so difficult, our spiritual good resolves so easily shattered, things not working out as we planned?

It is precisely *because* people don't behave according to our expectations, and because life *is* so complex, that we must let our Friend have as much of our thought as we possibly can. Time spent with Jesus always *saves* time. It saves time in fruitless effort, in bad relationships, in wrong decisions.

When you can create another few minutes to be alone with Him, here's a little reflection on what it means to *belong* to Jesus. Just lay aside all your concerns for a short time – and don't bother keeping rigidly to the words used here, of course:

Lord, I do thank You that I'm Yours ...

This means: *I'm secure.*

This means: *I can be free of unnecessary burdens – because I'm Your responsibility.*

This means: *You can't fail me.*

This means: *I must do all in my power not to fail You.*

This means: *You are at work in me – all the time.*

This means: *I need not strive – even in spiritual things!*

              Thank You again.

If time is limited, you can always leave your time of reflection unfinished, to be returned to later. You may not get past 'secure' – but there's no hurry!

One very important thing, which I'm sure you've realized: *times of thinking about Jesus are, of course, times when you are (consciously or unconsciously), absorbing what you see in Him.* We will think about this in a moment.

When on earth, our Lord was constantly misunderstood because of His consciousness of God the Father. The religious leaders diagnosed it as madness – or even worse. But Jesus never forgot the source of His life and His power. That is why He was the most perfectly balanced and really *sane* person we could ever find.

Jesus wants you to receive His life into your nature. He's going to be at work in such depth that you can't always distinguish between yourself and Him!

Jesus never wants to be just a helping agency. He wants to be our *life*. Now, this doesn't mean that we become mere ciphers, with our own personalities and talents disappearing. What Jesus our Lord does, in fact, is to make richer our real selves.

He shines through and enhances the good things He's already put into our natures. You're not John Brown cancelled out – but John Brown plus!

In our next chapter we're going to look at this process of 'absorbing' Jesus our Friend.

Lord,
It's exciting to think that I can share all that
You are. I know that it will help me such a
lot in the process of living in this very
uncertain world.

CHAPTER SEVEN

Just Absorbing!

Do you sometimes wish that you could change the present pattern of your life? Are you tempted to think that knowing Jesus would be so much easier in another environment, or another daily programme?

Well, I'm sure that you're beginning to realize that feeling closer to Him is possible in the most unlikely conditions. You may not need to run away from it all and become Brother Stephen or Sister Gillian!

If I were to ask each reader, 'How is the friendship of Jesus getting on?' I'd get some widely differing answers. This is because personalities vary so much (so did those of the first twelve of His disciples).

But if you've been putting into practice some of the things you've been reading, I know that you *will* have started to have a stronger sense of Jesus with you. And don't forget, there's no frantic rush. If your life is

48

based on Jesus – talking with Him, sharing everything with Him, 'receiving' from Him – a lifetime won't seem long enough even to begin to perfect it.

Nothing in the world is more exciting than Jesus sharing His life with you. It's marvellous how changes are made in you not always by great efforts of will-power, but just by being *in contact* with Him.

Receiving from Jesus has been described in many ways: a wire receiving its electricity, a branch receiving from the main tree, and so on. So you haven't got to ask Him, desperately, for this and that. All you have to do is to receive what is *yours* anyway – because you're living with Him.

This process doesn't have to wait until everything in your life has been sorted out. You begin receiving and absorbing *now*.

Drawing closer
One warning: don't look fussily, at frequent intervals, to see 'progress'. As long as you keep this in mind, you're going to surprise yourself. You're going to start acting in ways which once seemed beyond you. Your reactions to situations will be improving. You'll find that you're fonder of people.

Familiar things will give you more joy.
You'll be more controlled.

Looking at Jesus:
Thinking of all that He *is.*
Thinking of all that it means to *belong* to
    Him.
Letting yourself *absorb* from Him.

If you're allowing these things to happen for
the remainder of your life, you'll find that
you're becoming closer and closer to Him,
and increasingly enjoying His company.

Can you manage to do something every
day from now? Would you create a short
time for thinking of how the qualities you
see in Jesus really *are* becoming yours?
You'll be really surprised what this does for
you!

Try something like this:

Lord,
I think, gratefully, of all that I share,
if You are my Friend:

Your peace: *Thank You that it is*
growing in me.

Your patience: *Thank You that this is*
growing too!

Your compassion: *I share Your concern for*
others.

Your joy: *It doesn't depend on*
circumstances!

Your strength: *Thank You for a growing*
courage, in areas where I
used to be afraid.

Your wisdom: *It is helping me to make*
fewer mistakes.

Lord, thank You that I am making increasing
use of all that is mine – *united with You.*

The best way to use that last little reflection is to *linger* over each of those qualities: 'Lord, I have peace ... Your peace'; 'Lord, I have patience ... Your patience'. No hurry – just letting His life sink in! As with the other suggested reflections, you can easily break off in the middle if necessary, and continue when you've a few more spare minutes later on.

Recognizing what we are receiving, and thanking Him that we are doing so, means that we are able to go on absorbing, more and more, the life of God.

Look out, here's Adrian again! 'Haven't you heard the old maxim: "Work is prayer"? Surely, if you're busy on behalf of good causes, this is, in itself, an offering of worship to God.' Thanks, Adrian. There's truth in what you say. But like most half-truths, it can be misleading.

Please don't let people like Adrian or anyone else divert you from the indispensable thing, which is to 'be with' Jesus. Go on receiving from Him (even if you can only manage a few two-minute occasions during each day). You'll always feel glad that you had that time apart with Him. And you'll find that that very elusive thing, peace, is growing in you. It doesn't make your personality completely impervious to changes of mood, or to the effect difficult people sometimes have on you. But you'll find that the sense of calm stays around for much longer periods than it used to – as long as you keep your eyes upon your Friend!

Dear Lord,
Thank You that I am beginning to receive
into my nature all that You are.
When, from time to time I see progress,
let me be thankful rather than complacent
– knowing it's all due to You anyway.

CHAPTER EIGHT

Just Trusting!

Receiving all that Jesus has to share. It's a wonderful experience – especially if it happens within a life of complete trust in Him.

Complete trust?

That's asking a lot! Let's see what's involved.

We usually give complete trust to a human friend, if there's a deep affection, don't we? But there exists the sad situation that so many followers of Jesus manage to give Him only *partial* trust. Their sense of depending on Him at every moment isn't always very strong!

It's not easy to trust someone we can't see. So what we usually do is to give Him varying amounts of trust – while trying ever so hard, or impatiently, to shape events ourselves.

Not you again, Adrian! Go on, then: 'Well, look – does all this mean that if Jesus is our Friend, we can just sit back and do nothing to influence the details of our lives?' No, of course not, Adrian. It does mean, though, really *allowing* Him to work (which so many of you 'busy' Christians fail to do).

So often a person will say, 'Oh yes – all things are in His hands,' and then go on to plan so furiously and to make so many moves (not always very successfully).

Have you ever said a prayer about a difficult situation, which has then shown absolutely no improvement? Have you had to ask yourself, 'Is God really in control? Is He influencing this situation or not?'

It's as if you're challenged either to trust Him completely or not at all. Not easy is it? When things are bad, there's often a terrific pressure on us to give up trusting.

There's a conflict: 'This trust is getting me nowhere fast … or perhaps I really *should* give Him a chance.' And so … there may be a few hasty phone calls – or there may not!

What about ways of developing complete trust in Jesus?

One sure way is to think often about how *great* He is. Nothing is outside His control. Every possible combination of circumstances in your life He can shape.

As you do this, you soon find yourself quietly saying (in the most chaotic situations), 'It's in *Your* hands, Lord.'

You'll soon grow towards complete trust if you keep the concept of *Friend* very much in your mind. It's not simply that He chooses not to fail you – His friendship is such that He *can't*!

Remember this when things seem to be getting worse instead of better, or answers to your desperate prayers seem delayed. Yes, I know it's hard, but keep holding on to Jesus. He's not going to allow anything which, in the long term, could be disastrous for you.

Something else to remember is that He trusts *you*! He's not blind, of course, to your imperfections and many mistakes. And yet, those who follow Him soon get this feeling – that He trusts *them*. It's as if He were looking at you and saying, 'I know you can do it!'

Real trust

How else is real trust developed? You may have discovered already that it develops in life's frightening places, and in those shattering reverses. I meet so many people who, realizing there was literally no one who could really help, had to just throw themselves upon God.

When they did so they found how loving, how patient, and how much in control He was. And now they've a trust which you can't break!

The ingredients of a 'trust situation' between Jesus and yourself are:

1 His greatness.
2 Your patience.

That second one is hard isn't it? So often we're not aware of how He *is* at work – providing for us, working out complex situations for us. Later, though, we can see just what He's been doing.

Over and over again you'll be able to look back upon a pattern of events involving individuals, choices, chance meetings – which all combined to give the desired result. Every day, I'm amazed at the way He influences very difficult situations (or rather, I've stopped being amazed because He does it so often).

Because of His great love for you, Jesus our Lord will always *anticipate* what you need. He's already preparing what is required in your case. One verse in the Bible puts it very well: 'Before they call, I will answer!'

Another thing we learn as we start growing towards complete trust in Jesus is His *timing*. A course of action may seem right. A situation may seem greatly to be desired – but it has to be in His way, and in His time, to be most effective.

Adrian is bursting to come in: 'Surely, when a thing seems right, we have to do something; surely there are times when a choice has to be made pretty quickly? We can't just "leave it all to the Lord".'

Agreed, Adrian. There are many times when prompt action is called for. As long as there's a sense of His friendship, giving you an awareness of *when* to act decisively!

Let's suppose you've prayed about a situation, and a course of action seems both right and urgent. You can go ahead! But commit your action, and its consequences, to Him. And then *bring Him into* each developing pattern of circumstances. You must be prepared for Him to say, 'That's enough for the moment,' and accept it, when you're aware He is checking you. (*Events* often show us how He's allowing some things, but not others.)

Real patience is not the easiest thing to acquire is it? But if you're beginning to live close to Jesus, you're absorbing *His* patience, which should encourage you!

You'll find that Jesus is a Friend who deserves your *complete* trust at every stage of your life. I know that you're going to give Him this trust.

There will be many times when you'll look at the way things have been happening, and tell yourself how glad you are that you banked upon Him!

Dear Lord,
I realize that a growing trust is what follow-
ing You is all about. Help me to develop the
patience and the flexibility of one who knows
You are constantly at work on my behalf.
Thank You.

Another pause!
Having been reading about (and practising,
I hope!) things like reflecting, absorbing,
trusting, you've earned a breathing space.

As you look back on our book so far,
you'll have noticed how often Jesus's *love*
has been mentioned. This hasn't been to
give a nice 'tone' to the book. Far from it.
It's been mentioned so many times for a
definite reason. It's because being aware of
His love is the key to lots of areas which
people find very, very difficult.

Being conscious of His love is the
decisive factor in almost anything you can
think of. Things like:

· How you see the people around you
  – and the influence you have upon them.
· Your standards of behaviour – and how
  far you manage to live up to them!
· A *true* view of yourself.
· Answered prayers.
· A *deep* joy, contrasting with that 'bright-
  ness' which some Christians turn on –
  and which makes you want to run a mile!
· A real desire to please Jesus.

This awareness of His love finds its way into everything which can possibly happen to you on this planet.

There is still no need to hurry your reading. Go on thinking about His love. Allow plenty of time for experiment in real-life situations, based on what we've covered so far.

If you're making time for 'being with' Jesus your Friend, you can be sure that His love will become stronger than anything else in your experience. It will become the answer to everything.

And He's working, all the time, to bring you into a deeper relationship with Himself. Don't be one of those Christians who doesn't *allow* Him to work!

CHAPTER NINE

Secret Place

David is brought into hospital for the last few days of his life. He is in the terminal stages of a disease – and special drugs are ordered to help him.

David has always trusted Jesus. When the chaplain goes to see him, it's David who says the prayer – for them both!

We watch him getting weaker – but still showing no concern about his situation. He seems to be 'somewhere else' other than in the ward. No, he's not confused or drowsy – in fact very alert. The only way to describe it is that he is *protected*.

Eventually he dies. Then we learn that the drugs were never used. The nursing staff are amazed. David, with all sorts of undignified and uncomfortable things happening to his body, has been in what is sometimes called God's secret place. This is not a romantic creation of the imagination;

it's a place very real to those who know Jesus as Friend. As your trust in Jesus grows, I know that you'll increasingly use this place – *known just to you and Him.*

Many people who would never dream of calling it 'God's secret place', use it just the same! They instinctively go there when life becomes frightening or uncertain. It's not an escape from reality, by the way, because Jesus usually makes you *more* aware of the hard facts of life.

You've probably found that getting away from it all is never quite enough. It's hard to run away from yourself and your fears isn't it? But in this place in which the occupants are Jesus and yourself, you can start to relax a little, however difficult things are. You relax in what *He* is.

This secret place, shared with Jesus, becomes increasingly real as we make use of it. It can be used when alone in the mountains, it can be used when jostling round a supermarket. It's not just somewhere for times of crisis, but a place we get used to being in *at any time.* It doesn't matter how you personally visualize it, or what you call it, as long as you *use* it.

People often feel threatened, not only by influences from the world outside, but by things from their own minds. Not always easy to distinguish between the two sources! *But the answer is the same in each case.* Jesus is able to act as a protective shield in that deepest part of our being – our spirit. He protects that deepest part of us even from some of the strange things our mental processes get up to. I sometimes suggest to those who feel under pressure from a variety of frightening and negative thoughts, to picture Jesus coming between them and these things. I'm often told later how well this has worked. It works because they're not engaging in a naive exercise in auto-suggestion (which might horrify a self-respecting psychiatrist), but because Jesus is *actually doing* what they are trusting Him to do.

You probably know how it feels to have everything under control spiritually – prayers seem easier, sailing through temptations, God feeling closer. Then ... crash! There's a devastating crisis. Can we deal with it, or will it break us down completely?

However bad a person's situation (and yours could be pretty difficult right now), it's vital just to 'be with' Jesus in this place of His love. And then, through the remainder of the crisis, however long it may last, to continue there while He works – both in the situation and in you. You may have given that set of circumstances to Him mechanically at first, with very little hope. But increasingly the fact that He's in it with you is going to make all the difference. Being in a place shared just by Jesus, by the way, doesn't affect the way in which we share experiences with loved ones and others. What happens is that as we use this secret place, we become very different people in the way we *react* to life. We learn to keep the disturbing things *outside* His love.

Lord, help me to make increasing use of your secret place. Let me stay so close to You, that to be anywhere else seems unusual! From the place which I share with You, let me offer help to those who may themselves be passing through a very difficult time. Thank You.

CHAPTER TEN

Just Sharing!

Even as you're getting to know Jesus better, it sometimes happens that at the end of a day you have to admit something like this: 'I'm sure I haven't *really* helped anybody today. And as for being filled with joy and power … well!'

In other words, the day contained a lot which couldn't be put into the category either of truly giving or of truly receiving.

Let's risk annoying Adrian by one of those apparent oversimplifications: *Living with Jesus is all about being conscious of His love – and sharing it.*

'Now just a moment,' says Adrian, quick as a flash. 'Surely no one achieves a life filled with blissful meditation, going round giving out the love of Jesus to everyone in sight. Isn't it a little bit removed from reality?'

Well, Adrian, for many 'struggling Christians', it may seem just an ideal.

But the fact is that He wants us to fill our lives with as much as possible of *two things*: Ready?

1 *Receiving* from Him (about which we've said quite a lot already).
2 *Giving* (letting Him touch, or speak to others through us).

Sometimes a false contrast is made by Adrian and his friends. They see two groups of people: those living a life of prayer and meditation, and the others, who 'get things done'. You won't be taken in by this sort of thinking, I'm sure.

The only place from which you'll really begin to help others, and to bring some positive change in their lives is, in fact, the place of being conscious of Jesus's love. This doesn't mean, by the way, that when you're with other people you're trying, dreamily, to keep a sense of Jesus with you (more about this in a moment).

We find that time we've spent thinking about and talking with Jesus has not been a cosy, escapist indulgence, but an absolute necessity. From this place in His love, the greatest and most exciting thing we can do in this life starts to happen: our meetings with others, and our prayers for them, bringing the unique help of Jesus Himself!

Marvellous things happen when we're living close to Jesus. A hospital chaplain, for instance, soon learns that his own personality and the things he says or does at the patient's bedside are not the things which really change the patient's situation (even though God does, of course, use our personalities and gifts). What really matters is *keeping close* (i.e. being sure He's often in our thoughts). He said, 'Without Me, you can do nothing.' In other words, 'It's what I do, when you're united with Me, that's going to *last*.'

In His way
First of all, then, don't rely only on your reason, your careful planning, or your bursts of enthusiasm, in setting out to 'share' Jesus your Friend. It's far, far better just to be surrendered to Him, prepared to be very flexible in the way He uses you. Otherwise there may be great activity in a certain direction, with very little achieved!

Just a word spoken to someone as we live close to Jesus, ready to be used as *He* wishes, can change that person's situation more than many thoughtfully planned schemes. *Jesus* is in that word!

Never forget that what each follower of Jesus can give to others is going to be very different. You may be able to tear round the wards of a hospital, but you could, instead, be confined to a wheelchair and only 'share' Him with one other person during an entire week. It doesn't matter! He only wants you to promise Him that, as far as possible, the lives (even if only one or two) which touch yours, will be made brighter.

We never have to look round (once we've made that promise) for people to help. He confronts us with them! And often they're people close to us, whose needs we've never noticed before.

Remember that even while you're still 'only growing' in a sense of Jesus's friendship, He'll be using you. Even while you feel how inadequate you are, He'll be using you. Just as long as you've put yourself at His disposal!

Just what is it that *Jesus* does which is so much more effective than our eloquence, good intentions, strategy? Well, it's not merely that Jesus in you makes you a shining *example* to the world. Something else is happening. There's a very definite *influence* from Him – through you.

Christians often forget that not only is He 'with us' but with us to be *used*. He longs to be, through us, a dynamic influence. In any situation where Jesus is *allowed* to work, this influence exists. I'm always seeing very agitated people suddenly become calm and start to talk hopefully – not through any words of mine, but because Jesus is there with us!

Here's something you might like to do (if you've not done it so far) about contacts you have with people. Ask Jesus our Lord to help you to see them through *His* eyes of love – *and He will*. Then thank Jesus, in sheer trust, that *something is happening* between Him and the person you're with.

A doctor, nurse, minister, social worker, or anyone in frequent contact with broken-hearted, frightened people, can't ask God for any better gift than that of love. It's *His* love with which we now love others – our

own may be a bit selective or unpredictable!
And so you, in your own unique circumstances and with your own unique opportunities, are always wise to ask first for His
love to be in you. We know, don't we, how
often a mum literally 'loves' her child better?

Mr A., who *loves*, is going to help someone more than even Mr B., that prominent
charismatic figure, of powerful faith, praying equally powerfully!

Being conscious of Jesus, by the way,
doesn't mean that you're performing mental
gymnastics. You're not trying to concentrate
upon a friend and, at the same time, strain-
ing to contemplate *Him*. (Your acquaintance would rightly be annoyed if he knew.)
It simply means that the other person gets
your full and loving attention, but at the
same time never far away, there is an
awareness of just whose Presence you are
in. One of the many things which Jesus our
Lord does so well is helping us to be aware
of Him – *without anything less going to the
other person.*

He's in it

What you've tried to share with someone
may seem a bit trivial. It may be a smile or

a quick, reassuring comment. But He will be in it.

So thank Him from time to time for what He did in your encounters with other people, even if you're not always conscious of just what He *did* do!

A smile has often stopped a potential suicide, and that reassuring remark of yours (especially if Jesus is part of it) can go right through a darkness which you never dreamed existed.

Have you been thinking that 'Jesus reaching others through us' isn't quite the whole story? You're right. When we act lovingly towards people, *He* receives too – that's how closely He is identified with us. I know that it's a bit hard to visualize, but never forget how much He is *involved* in this interaction of human beings – involved in both the 'giving' and 'receiving' capacities! That's why we must never feel smug in our private relationship with Him, and perhaps be acting coldly, or deprivingly, to someone close to us – not realizing that we're hurting Him too.

There's always a temptation to forget that Jesus not only works through you but *for* you. He really *is* helping those you say a prayer for – often without your contact with them. And He completes (in a perfect way) those imperfect 'practical' things you attempt for Him.

By the way, although Jesus wants to be able to depend on you in the important things each day, He wants you also to enjoy His gifts and His world! Many very kind Christian people, including some clergy and ministers, temporarily forget this, and then break down completely. He's not merely a Friend whose company we can learn to enjoy – He enjoys *ours*. And so, you are 'doing something' for Him when you take time just to be with Him, to enjoy Him, and to enjoy His creation.

Life can't be boring when you know that Jesus is *at work* through you. He lifts your encounters with others into a completely new dimension.

Because He's sharing life with you, you can be absolutely sure that no time you spend with someone else is being wasted.

Dear Lord,
I would like Your love to flow,
more and more, to everyone I meet.
May what I say, or do,
each visit I make, each letter I write,
each prayer I say,
make a difference *to someone's life.*
Thank You.

CHAPTER ELEVEN

When It All Goes Wrong

'Say something nice to everyone you meet today – it'll drive 'em crazy.'

So says one of those colourful posters with which youngsters often adorn their bedroom doors.

It reminds us, of course, that our best intentions can so easily fail.

Everything getting streamlined in living close to Jesus, and then – crash! We find we've hurt someone, or we've scored a great miss somewhere. 'Your religion doesn't do much for *you*,' says an acquaintance, and bump we go.

The pressures on those who share life with Jesus, and look like being useful to Him, can be subtle. Many occur in that tricky sphere, relationships (e.g. within families).

Things like pride, anger, lack of patience, crop up just here don't they?

There's no more difficult part of life than that of getting along with others – including, of course, those closest to us!

Factors influencing our relationships are, as you know, complex. There can be clashes of basic temperament, ignorance of our own and others' behaviour motivations, two people pursuing entirely different objectives, and other influences which we can't always detect.

Is advice enough?
Let's say that twelve writers set out what they saw as important about living with other people.

Provided that you could endure all this advice, you'd be awfully confused by the end of it, and probably feel like banging your head against a convenient wall.

The writers would probably cover self-evident things, like the need for patience, putting others at ease, not manipulating or exploiting others, trying to see another's viewpoint, jumping on pride, being more ready to listen, acting lovingly when not feeling inclined to do so – and so on.

Those writers knowing some psychology would step in with insights into the motivations of your actions, help in more deeply understanding people (so that you aren't constantly angry or disappointed in your expectations of them), and help in understanding yourself, and the unconscious pressures upon you.

I'm sure you'd find it all helpful in avoiding many mistakes and yet there'd be something missing wouldn't there? *Failures would still be happening in relationships!* You'd feel like saying, as that honest man Paul did: 'I don't do what I want, but, instead, keep doing the things I hate.' Today Paul might have said: 'Here I am, mentally equipped by ethical and psychological teaching, to make a real success of living – but I keep putting my foot in it!'

You'd get very discouraged if it wasn't for that thing we thought about earlier – the *influence* of Jesus. Make sure that your encounters with people are under this influence (which they are if He's in your thoughts a lot). Jesus has a wonderful way of neutralizing 'contra-influences' and incompatibilities.

Talking of 'contra-influences', many

believe, of course, that it's not just chemical make-up, or earliest experiences affecting our relationships. In addition to God's influence (producing reasonableness, unselfishness, patience) there is the influence of supernatural evil, (seeking to produce mistrust, resentment, intolerance, and even, of course, murderous anger).

I know that in some places today it's not fashionable to think this way! But Jesus our Lord was *very* sure about this pressure on us by evil, wasn't He? And because He saw it for what it was (because He made the right diagnosis), He had a unique success rate in making people happy and well again, didn't He? But never mind for the moment the true source of negative influences. The vital thing to remember is that *God has the answer to them.*

By the way, don't get like Mr A. who blames supernatural evil for *everything* that goes wrong, instead of taking responsibility himself! Involved in a stormy relationship, Mr A. soothes himself with the thought: 'This is all happening because I'm a Christian, and the other person isn't.'

Well, of course, it's true that if you follow Jesus, it's going to arouse antagonism.

He warned us that it would. There are times when you're disliked or misunderstood for trying to do God's will – and only kept going by the thought that at least *He* understands.

But it's dangerous to go on to assume that people's hostility is always aroused by *our* goodness!

Disharmony! Could you possibly be in such a state with someone right now? At least you know how it feels. One disharmony can darken the whole of your life, can't it?

And a hurt-feeling situation occurs so unexpectedly doesn't it? Often there's no immediate opportunity to 'put things right'.

The *only* thing we can do is to bring this to Jesus our Friend until such an opportunity comes. We bring to Him the other person – and the situation.

You won't be surprised, of course (especially if you've tried it), that this works wonderfully. I've seen so many people 'made friends' (much better than they were previously) because someone *prayed*. It's just as well that we don't always get that opportunity to 'sort it out' with the other person in our own way! It's all part of our Friend being *allowed* to exert His influence – being given space in which to work! The old advice about getting out of a room and praying before a quarrel gets worse is very sound.

Does what I've just said sound a little too good to be true? It would be wrong to pretend that you *always* see immediate results, but patience and trusting restraint work wonders. You'll find that 'bringing Jesus in', as an automatic thing, works miraculously in hurts and misunderstandings.

Resentments! Christians will quickly agree that it's 'harmful to have them' but, oh dear, how often, when we talk to a Christian, we find a *huge* resentment lurking!

Here's something you can do if there's a resentment lurking in you. Ready? Look at the resentment-causing situation with your intellect, rather than the emotions – as if you were an interested third party! Give the resentment to Jesus your Friend. Let His love, in you, dissolve it. Ask Him to do what you may find it hard to do. Ask Him to bless the other person. Yes, you'll find that you really do want something good to happen to Mrs B. who treated you so badly! A relationship is on the way to being mended – with someone living or dead.

By the way, hurts and resentments can largely be prevented from ever intruding in the first place. What you do is to mentally 'set people free' (you no longer demand nor expect from them, gratitude, praise, recognition, or their supposed 'duty' towards you).

When things go wrong, have you tried 'seeing' the other person and yourself, together, in the light of God's love? See other influences excluded (and then *hold* to that picture). You'll usually see an improvement. These are sometimes dramatic, sometimes gradual – we're not always aware of why some take longer than others!

Bringing Jesus into every relationship and allowing Him to work isn't some 'way-out' form of Christianity. It's *normal* Christianity in one of its very neglected aspects.

It's no wonder that so many 'believers' don't feel Him very close when they leave Him out of things so much.

You wouldn't want a long and very obvious list of those temptations and 'pressures' which can cause any day to go wrong. And so the only one I'll mention is spiritual pride – because it's the most sinister! The big danger is to see ourselves as 'super-Christians' compared with others, and to forget that all our 'progress' is due to God anyway. Fortunately, He often lets us see ourselves entering this state: 'There I go again Lord – I'm sorry. Knock this out of me for good.'

You'll win!

Just as temptations and pressures differ widely, so will the ways you personally find helpful in overcoming them. What often happens is that, through habit, you're caught off guard and find you've already begun a wrong pattern of thinking or con-versation. Never mind! Just glance to Jesus and *refuse the deliberate continuance* of that pattern. And so the next comment to your companion at the breakfast table could be one of compliment rather than criticism! With Jesus it works. Try it.

By the way, don't forget the value of the *pause* when under pressure to commit yourself to some wrong word or action. St Paul called it the way of escape. The longer the pause (taking a good look at Jesus as we do), the weaker becomes the pressure on us.

The feeling of being united with Jesus is marvellous in sailing through those things which used to knock you for six.

Lord,
I realize that people won't always behave in the way I expect – often I'll be disappointed in them. And, often, I'll be disappointed in myself! Help me to use You, in every kind of pressure which would deflect me from the way which pleases You.
I'll remember to bring You in – straight away – when everything goes terribly wrong.

Love – all the time

Would you like to acquire a habit which will change, dramatically, the way you live? You would? Well, start to think about Jesus's love as *surrounding* all that you do. See everything (alone or with others) as happening in the context of that love – a way of thinking which will become automatic.

Here's a list you can go through in His presence whenever there's an opportunity (take your time over it):

Dear Lord,
I remind myself of all that results from consciously living in Your love:

· In Your love, I need not fear anything
  – nor need I ever act out of fear.
· In Your love, I can be very patient.
· In Your love, I'm able to keep a quiet joy
  – even when everything is difficult or threatening.
· In Your love, my love for You keeps growing.
· In Your love, I'm learning serenity, and I'm not 'trying' so frantically!
· In Your love, I'm instinctively refusing what I know would hurt that love.
· In Your love, there's a healing influence upon every part of me.
· In Your love, Your work of drawing me closer to Yourself goes on continuously.

Thank You.

CHAPTER TWELVE

Just Reflecting!

'I wish I could be more like Jesus,' sighed a young man who had recently taken a revealing look at himself.

Well, he needn't worry, because in a world of increasing specialization, there's one very difficult skill possessed by Jesus our Friend. It's that of changing *people*.

Do you know the best thing that anyone can ever think about you? It's that they can see *Jesus* in you. But it's better, of course, if they don't tell you! Don't listen to Adrian or anyone who claims that there's any 'Christian activity' more important than reflecting Jesus. If you're reflecting Him, it won't make you say: 'I've made great progress in being virtuous.' But it will make an agnostic friend think: 'There's something in Christianity after all!'

And so, how does it all start – the exciting process of Jesus changing us, so that *He* is reflected in us?

Well, you've found already that being aware of His love makes you genuinely sorry about anything in your life which may be hurting Him. It makes you want, desperately, to do better. You develop a 'being sorry' potential. Does this sound a bit morbid? It isn't really.

What Jesus does is to give you *realism*. You'll see your progress – OK! But you'll see one or two things urgently needing to be put right. A few not-so-good tendencies could have crept in lately alongside those 'spiritual advances'!

The ideal starting point in the change process is when we start to say: 'Lord, make me aware of anything so habitual that I never dream it's hurting You.' A lot of long-established Christians could do with asking this!

Yes – a new person!

Have you noticed something about the list which Jesus gave of the happy people? There were, of course, the peacemakers, the merciful, the humble minded.

But there's one group different from the rest. It's this: 'Happy are those who are hungry and thirsty for goodness.' Aren't you glad He found room for it? No 'attainment' mentioned – it's just the *wish* to change which He sees as a virtue in itself!

So how about this wish being *your* steady intention? He sees it when you only see your failures.

Don't forget:

1 The *wish* to be someone Jesus is pleased with.
2 Forgetting about the process, as far as possible. (He'll allow you glimpses of your progress, so don't worry.)

He'll be making you into a *new person*, even if you're looking in vain for changes right now!

Here's something to realize. While you've been thinking about Jesus, letting Him work in you, many things about you have been changing. You probably think that most things haven't altered. But there's one basic test: Do I want to please Him now, where once I wanted to please myself? Do I? Do I?

Is the thoughtful answer 'Yes'? If so, He's definitely creating a new person in your case!

Here's something which will help along the change process. Say to Him at odd times during each day, 'Lord, just what *You* want' (or words to the same effect). Smile when you do so! Don't have a grim stoical 'acceptance' – as if what He wants for you must be something awful!

This will put you on to a sort of 'obedience wavelength' – doing the right things without even thinking about them.

'A lot of talk about Jesus changing us. What about *our* effort?' (Yes, Adrian again.)

Well, I often find things happening (after bringing to Him problem situations), where I haven't done a thing – except tell Him about it! But our Adrian has a point. Jesus does look for *our* effort in many cases, and then influences that effort towards success.

Do you think He might be looking for an effort from you in giving up one or two things which are preventing you from really enjoying Him?

Don't forget that in place of what goes, He'll always give you something far, far better.

Have you been thinking, 'What about those times when I want to act like a new person, but find a tremendous pressure in the opposite direction?'

There's only one thing to do at such times. Very deliberately look to your Friend, Jesus, to literally *take you through* the making of that choice. It often involves an effort – but He'll always complete your effort successfully.

The more closely united you are with Jesus, the more aware you'll be of the way to take in tricky decisions – provided you're doing what pleases Him in those other things where the right course *is* clear.

It's happening

Jesus said He wanted you to be a light in this confusing world. He didn't mean that you were to perform certain duties, very self-consciously, hoping other people would see Him in you! He just wants you to let Him live and work through you, so that His light is automatically reflected – with you probably unaware of it.

Don't get worried if you start noticing even more differences between Jesus and you. That's progress. Keep looking in His direction, rather than at yourself to 'see' changes. You'll soon know that things are happening – you'll be saying, 'Yes, I *know* I'm calmer. I *know* I'm more controlled. I *know* I'm more at ease with people. I *know* I'm not upset by the things which used to upset me.'

By the way, don't throw away (in a careless moment or under temporary pressure) gains you've made. Going back to square one can usually be avoided, with just a little more firmness, and His help guaranteed!

Climbers who have negotiated dizzy ice-walls with experienced guides have described a definite feeling about those leading them. It's a deep sense of companionship – and it's all produced by carrying out their guide's directions!

If you want to reflect Jesus, He makes you a promise (you'll find it in John's Gospel). He says that if you let Him lead you, and change your reactions, you'll start to 'live in His love'. In other words, you'll not only be changing – but you'll have a strong sense of His companionship.

'Special offers' are tempting aren't they? Jesus makes a marvellous one: 'Accept a fairly easy "burden" (that of pleasing Me), and I'll let you unload on to Me your often huge burdens and problems.' In other words: 'Just carry out My wishes and leave Me to handle yours.'

It isn't just strong and confident people who 'arrive' at living harmoniously with Jesus and reflecting Him. Success also comes to those who battle along very unsurely, very apologetically, and with lots of failures. You?

Jesus never goes on strike when you fail. He doesn't get discouraged and give up, provided you go on *wanting* to be more like Him. He'll always pick you up after failures. He'll take you on to levels where your wishes harmonize with His – and *His* reflection in you gets brighter and brighter!

Dear Lord,
I know I can trust You to make me the sort
of person who reflects You. If there is lurking
in me any area of reluctance to change,
please help me to deal with it.
Thank You.

CHAPTER THIRTEEN

Fact-Based Prayer

Imagine that you possess a listening device, and overheard the prayer of someone who tries to keep as close as possible to Jesus each day.

That prayer probably mentioned certain *facts* about the relationship with Him. And that's vital! If you don't remind yourself of these facts every day, what you say to Him is going to depend far too much on fluctuating moods. In some moods, praying is about the last thing you feel like doing.

In case you'd like to borrow any of it, a 'facts prayer' is printed overleaf. I know you'll keep the content flexible (according to circumstances) and that you'll increasingly express thoughts from here in a way which makes them your own.

It won't be all talking, of course. Jesus will give you a *very* clear awareness about certain things if you 'listen'.

Always use this facts-based contact with your Friend (however you may be feeling). It has tremendous results. He gradually becomes so real to you that wherever you are, whatever you're doing, you just take His presence for granted!

Lord, I thank You for these facts:
· *Thank You that you chose me.*
· *Thank You that I belong to You – always.*
· *Thank You that I have the greatest of life's gifts – Yourself!*
· *Thank You for Your care through my life so far – providing for me, protecting me (often without my realizing it).*
· *Thank You for all that You have 'sent' or 'permitted' in my life – because You have made it all harmonize with Your good purposes.*
· *Thank You for all my present blessings.*
· *Thank You for a growing experience of your very wonderful love.*

Here are more outlines of other suggested prayers – no need for them to be used all at once!

Lord, I'm sorry:
- *Sorry for the many times I've failed You.*
- *Sorry that I've not always used the strength which would have enabled me to do so much better.*
- *Sorry for wrong tendencies in me which I have been slow to reverse, with Your help.*
- *Sorry for everything that has hurt your love – and Your expectations of me.*
  Please forgive me.

Lord, may Your will be done:
- *I trust You to over-rule any initiatives of mine which are contrary to Your will – and to add Your blessing to those things which are pleasing to You.*
- *I surrender myself completely to You, this and every day, so that what You want may happen in my life.*
- *Let me see Your will more and more clearly – so that I don't 'slow down' its working out.*
- *Thank You that Your wishes are being carried out in my present circumstances.*

Lord, please help:
- *Those who are very frightened.*
- *Those who are broken hearted, and see no purpose in living.*
- *Those who are unwanted.*
- *Those who are misunderstood.*
- *Those who have no food, shelter, security, in the world today.*
- *Those with no faith.*
- *My loved ones and others I now name before You.*
- *All those known to You who are in great need at this time.*
- *Please show me what I can do to best help those around me, and advance Your purposes.*

Lord, I receive:
Because I am united with You, and share Your life, I thank You for some more facts!
I'm growing: in love, Your love;
in peace, Your peace;
in patience, Your patience;
in wisdom, Your wisdom;
in true joy, Your joy.

> *Lord, I thank You and praise You:*
> · *For all that You are.*
> · *For all that You have done for me (I owe everything to You).*
> · *For all that You now mean to me.*
> · *I praise You, Lord Jesus, my Friend.*
> · *I praise You, heavenly Father, so close to me in Jesus, my Lord.*

Those needing help

In the 'Lord, please help' part, what is the most effective way to pray for someone we know to be in need?

There are many approaches to this and, as you know, entire books have been devoted to the subject.

I'm sure that many of your own prayers for others will now be springing naturally from a growing trust in Jesus our Lord, and a growing concern about people around you. Because of this, they're likely to be answered prayers.

We should never prescribe for God what the person really needs (which is what we're often tempted to do), nor think that His response depends on our intensity, on any technique, or on our flow of beautiful words.

By now, we're used to thinking about the love of Jesus, aren't we? Well, just imaginatively hold up the person who needs help *in that love*.

We noticed Susan at the office today. When we spoke to her she was tense, on the verge of tears. She didn't want to say too much about the causes of what was bothering her – and what we said to her seemed so feeble and inadequate.

At the first opportunity we 'bring' Susan to Jesus our Friend: 'Lord, please bless Susan. *You* know what's wrong. Please give to her what she really needs.'

And what should we be *wanting* for Susan? Above everything else, we should want her to experience the companionship of Jesus! As we pray for Susan, He may make us very aware of something more He wants *us* to do for her.

Don't forget that a prayer said *before* or *after* being with people is equally effective. For instance, if we know we're going to meet someone, the meeting should, ideally,

fit into what the Lord is *already doing* about
that encounter, because we've prayed!

Let's say we met Andrew unexpectedly,
and tried to say or do something helpful on
the spur of the moment. The *important*
thing is still the prayer we say about
Andrew afterwards!

And, of course, you'll remember to *thank*
Him during the days which follow, for what
He's doing in Andrew's life and for each
person for whom you've prayed.

I'm pretty sure that prayer is no longer,
for you, the frightening word it is for some.
Prayer of any kind (as long as it isn't
mechanical).

Any kind – praising, feeling ashamed,
being grateful, being submissive, seeking
guidance, concerned for other people. It's
all making a very strong link between Jesus
and you – a link which isn't going to break!

His gift
I'm sure you've noticed how much Jesus's
peace is becoming part of you. You notice
this when it's temporarily lost for some
reason, don't you?

The sense of calm has grown if you've been 'with Him' a lot – and sharing even the smallest details with Him.

Don't forget that Jesus wants you to have that peace, not just at certain periods, but uninterruptedly.

It's helpful, whenever you can, to make a short time for focusing on His peace. Something like this:

Dear Lord,
Even the thought of You brings peace.
The thought of Your constant concern for
me. The thought of how great You are.
Your peace is a barrier against all that's
harmful. And it's at work inside me, too.
Right now, I rest in its influence.
May I carry Your peace with me.
May it pass to those I meet!
Thank You again.

Start of a Journey

We're almost at the end of our book, but only in the early stages of what's going to be an often-breathtaking journey – with Jesus.

There will be moments when you're tempted to think that it's all been a waste of time. Just resist that temptation, because you'll find that life shared with Jesus is *every bit as wonderful as described.*

His friendship won't clash with your human friendships – on the contrary, it's going to do such a lot for them.

Do you have a fairly solitary existence? His presence is going to bring you courage. It's going to give you something to hope for. It's going to bring a sense of not being alone for a single moment.

This is a good time to ask Him to make you aware of anything upon which you should be concentrating right now.

If you've found the book helpful, I'm glad! But I'll be delighted if you now make the suggestions for times of quiet (and other parts you've found helpful) part of your way of life.

By now you've realized that you don't have to keep a lot of rules in order to hold on to Jesus, but here are some reminders of things which (from your side) will help to *deepen* the friendship. I'm sure that some have already become automatic.

Here they are:

· Offering each day to Him. Thank Him that He's going to bless and use the day – and He will.

· Ignoring Adrian and creating brief times in which to do nothing except to think of Jesus – and to take in all that He has to share.

· Thanking Him, often, for what He's doing (even in the absence of anything tangible).

· Making a regular time to look at Him in action in the Bible and to let His words shape the way you live. Taking a good look at God's *promises* in the Bible and applying them to *you*. Remember that as you let in God's word in this way, you're letting in Himself!

· A word, or just a look, of *trust* – even when busy.

· *Noticing* the needs of people around you – and letting His love reach them through you.

· Seeing temptations which hit you, not as things to be 'struggled against', but as things to be despised!

· Asking His help for those *He* knows to be in great need of that help – at the time you're praying. You can be sure that He's making use of that prayer – usually for people you're never likely to meet!

· Sharing the hopes and the problems of others who are learning to know Jesus. It's still a world which largely ignores Him, and He wants those like you, who *are* interested, to be together – a real part of Himself. So don't be afraid to get really involved in a church!

· Telling Him, from time to time, of your love and your trust (however imperfect you still consider them to be). You're going to be among that minority who make God glad – by loving Him *for His own sake*. 'Ministering' to Him!

There will be days when you can't carve out as much time as you'd like to be 'with Him'. Don't worry, you can take it for granted that He's constantly thinking of all that concerns you!

Finally
On this journey with Jesus I know you won't be surprised if there are some tremendous conflicts, all sorts of problems (some of a type never encountered before), and, inevitably, some very sad times.

But I also know that you'll be keeping firmly in your mind that you have precisely the same Friend who has meant everything to the great saints throughout history.

Do you know something?

It means everything to Jesus that you're now part of Him. And it means everything to Him that you're on His side.

The friendship of Jesus is yours. Your Friend wants you to *use* Him, increasingly.

He's actually living in you – so don't waste Him, will you?

He is *enjoying* you!

Jesus says: 'Live in Me – and I in you.'

Dear Lord,
I believe that what now exists between us is going to last for ever. I know that things won't always be easy – but I have You, the Saviour of the world, as my companion. I trust completely in all that You are and I look forward to what I can become, united with You! For the remainder of my life I want to share every experience with You. In the working out of Your plan for this world, You can count on me.

His promise: 'I am with you – always.'

Also from John Woolley

I AM WITH YOU

Since 1984 people throughout the world have
been discovering the power to change lives of
the little devotional book, *I Am With You*.

The divinely inspired words bring a sense
of our Lord's presence, in a wonderful way, to
strengthen the reader in his or her personal
need.

I commend this little book to all who are seeking
to deepen their spiritual lives.
– Cardinal Basil Hume, England

I Am With You *is a very special book;*
it will bless countless people.
– Prebendary John Pearce, England

I have never experienced such a
closeness to Jesus.
– Fran Gunning, USA

A lovely book of devotions; we use it daily.
– Dr Donald English,
former President, Methodist Conference

I Am With You *will deeply touch many people.*
– Fr. Robert de Grandis, USA

The most wonderful book I have ever read.
– Fr. Tom Cass, England